Getting To Know...

Nature's Children

WILD HORSES

Martin Harbury

GROLIER
BOOKS

Facts in Brief

Classification of North American wild horses

    Class: *Mammalia* (mammals)

    Order: *Perissodactyla* (odd-toed hoofed mammals)

    Family: *Equidae* (horse family)

    Genus: *Equus*

    Species: *Equus caballus* (same species as the domestic horse)

Habitat. Forests, plains, deserts, mountains, and valleys.

Distinctive physical characteristics. Smaller than most domestic horses; usually has a stripe down the middle of the back, and dark stockings.

Habits. Lives in bands; is shy. Sometimes wild horses groom each other.

Diet. Grasses, shrubs, roots, and twigs.

Edited by: Elizabeth Grace Zuraw
Design/Photo Editor: Nancy Norton
Photo Rights: Ivy Images

ISBN: 0-7172-6450-5

Have you ever wondered . . .

When you think of horses, what do you picture in your mind?

- beautiful, long-legged race horses
- strong, plodding workhorses pulling carts
- well-trained police horses
- gentle saddle ponies
- stubborn mules loaded with backpacks?

Or do you think of wild horses?

People have always been fascinated by horses. They've written books about them, such as *Black Beauty* and *My Friend Flicka,* and made movies about them, such as "The Black Stallion." But perhaps the most interesting horses are wild horses, sometimes called *mustangs.*

There are groups of wild horses in many places around North America. If you're lucky, someday you may get to see one. But if you do, it will almost surely be from a distance. Wild horses are very shy and don't let people get close. If they sense anyone nearby, they speed away and are gone in the blink of an eye.

The Horse Family History

If wild horses held a family picnic, it would be a most unusual gathering. There'd be lots of close cousins—zebras, donkeys, asses (wild, untamed donkeys), and every kind of saddle, race, and cart horse. But that's not all. The wild horse's more distant cousins include the rhinoceros and the tapir!

Horses have been around since the time of the dinosaurs. One of their earliest ancestors, called *Eohippus,* didn't look like today's horse. It was about the size of a fox. Being small made it easier for it to escape dinosaurs by scampering under bushes. Another difference was in the feet. Instead of hoofs, *Eohippus* had pads with several toes.

Dinosaurs died out—they probably didn't adapt when the weather changed. But the horse family didn't become *extinct,* or go out of existence. Horses changed and grew through the ages until they came to look like the horses of today.

Once all horses were wild. But then people began to trap and tame them. Now there are only a few wild horses left.

In the early 1900s, more than 2 million mustangs roamed the West. Today only about 20,000 exist.

Horses in North America

The story of all North American horses is an old and interesting one. Long, long ago, horses lived in the wild in most parts of North America. But between 8,000 and 10,000 years ago, they all died out. Horses didn't reappear again until about 400 years ago when the Spanish explorers brought some with them from Europe.

Other Europeans who followed brought more horses, and soon the Native Americans started to raise and use horses, too. Many of the horses escaped onto the prairies where the climate and grass suited them well. Before long, thousands of wild horses were running free, becoming more and more like their wild ancestors.

All North American mustangs are descended from *domestic,* or tame, horses. The only true wild horse in the world is the Przewalski horse, which once lived along the China-Mongolian border. It is extinct in its original home, but it can still be found in zoos and preserves around the world.

Opposite page:
The Assateague Pony descends from ponies that got established along the coasts of Virginia and Maryland some-time after the discovery of America. Its ancestors may have been washed ashore from a shipwrecked Spanish vessel.

Where to Look for Wild Horses

The largest number of mustangs live in the deserts of Nevada. Deserts aren't this animal's preferred *habitat,* or place where an animal naturally lives. But our expanding cities and farms haven't left wild horses much choice. Fortunately, mustangs are adaptable. They manage to survive on sagebrush and other desert food and on the meager trickles of water found at a few watering spots.

Other wild horses live in the Pryor Mountains of Montana and Wyoming, where the canyons, rivers, forests, and meadows provide all of the mustangs' favorite foods. And the area offers the shy animals plenty of places to hide.

Pryor Mountain mustangs may be shy, but they're also very curious. In fact, if you tried to sneak up on them, you might suddenly feel as if *you* were being watched. Often mustangs turn the tables on people by sneaking around to follow them from behind. But as soon as the horses are spotted, they dash away!

The Sable Islanders

Sable Island is a large, sandy island that rises out of the Atlantic Ocean off the coast of Canada's Nova Scotia. This remote spot is an unlikely place to find anything but seagulls, sand dunes, and fish. But there also are some more unusual finds on Sable Island.

Ipswitch Sparrows fly from as far south as Georgia to lay their eggs on Sable Island, hundreds of shipwrecks litter the island's shores, and only a few people live there to look after the lighthouses and the weather station. But the most curious thing about Sable Island is that 300 wild horses make their home there!

In fact, the tough little Sable Island horses have been there for hundreds of years. No one really knows how they got there, but some people think that the first horses were survivors that swam ashore after a shipwreck.

Sable Island wild horses find plant food along the Atlantic shore.

Winter Storms, Summer Playground

Life isn't easy for the wild horses of Sable Island, especially in winter, when ferocious storms bring stinging ice and snow and chilling winds. Then the little horses huddle behind the sand dunes for shelter. They grow long thick coats to keep out the cold. Sometimes, they have to break through ice to get water to drink, or dig through the snow and sand to find hidden grass shoots.

But in the summer when the sun's warmth beams down, the horses shed their long, woolly winter coats. Food becomes plentiful as the green grass grows fresh again and the ponds fill up with water. Then the Sable Island horses can be carefree, spending their days munching on sweet grass and running along the long, beautiful beaches.

The wild horses that live in northern regions may be small, but they're strong and hardy, capable of weathering harsh winter storms.

Small Cousins

Wild horses are smaller than most of their domestic cousins. This is because the food they eat in the wild isn't as nutritious as the special foods and hay that people feed to domestic horses. If a baby wild horse, or *foal,* is caught very young and fed domestic foods, it will grow at least a hand taller than either of its parents. A *hand* is the unit used to measure the height of a horse. A hand is equal to the width of an average adult man's hand: 4 inches (10 centimeters).

Much of the difference in height between a wild horse and a domestic horse is in the *foreleg,* or front leg. This works out very well for the wild horse because shorter bones are stronger. Thanks to its short, strong bones, a wild horse is less likely to break a leg if one of its *hoofs,* or feet, slips into a hole.

Most wild horses are only between 12 and 14 hands at the shoulder, or between 48 and 56 inches (122 and 142 centimeters) tall. Sable horses, however, are considerably smaller than this.

Opposite page: *Wild horses are often referred to as* feral, *a word used to describe animals that return to the wild state after having been tame.*

Coats of Many Colors

Wild horses come in various colors. They can be black or white or different shades of brown, tan, or gray. Some are all one color, others are dappled.

Over many years, as horses lived in the wild, many of them began to acquire special markings, including dark lower legs and a dark stripe down the back from the mane to the tail. A *mane* is the long, heavy hair that grows around the neck of some animals. Sometimes, like zebras, wild horses might have little dark strips called *fingermarks* on their upper legs. These markings are good *camouflage*—they help the animals blend in with their surroundings, making it more difficult for their enemies to see them.

Long ago, different Native American tribes favored horses with certain markings. The Cheyenne, for example, liked horses that they called Medicine Hat. These horses had white coats with special, darker markings on their heads and chests. The Cheyenne believed that these markings, which looked a bit like a war bonnet and a chest shield, helped protect both horse and rider.

Pinto is the name for a horse with spots. These Medicine Hat pintos
have dark bonnets and chest patches that are plain to see.

Protective Hair

Horses that live in cold climates grow a thick winter coat every autumn and don't shed it until spring. But they never shed their mane and tail hairs.

In spring and summer when there are lots of pesky bugs around, the horses use their tails as fly swatters to swish the insects away. If that doesn't work, the horses have special muscles under their skin that they can twitch to get rid of the insect pests.

Scratch and Clean

Horses love to *groom,* or clean, themselves, and they have some unusual ways of keeping their coats tidy and their skin free from itches. A favorite way is to roll on the ground on their backs. They roll on grass or in water or in a patch of dust or even in mud! If they find a really good rolling spot, several horses may take turns scratching their backs by rolling in it.

Horses also like to rub their heads and necks against fences, rocks, or trees. And sometimes they may scratch themselves with their hoofs or sharp front teeth.

Opposite page: *These wild horses in the Pryor Mountains have grown thick coats for the winter.*

You Scratch My Back...

Sometimes two horses help each other groom spots that they can't reach by themselves. They use their teeth to nibble along each other's manes and necks and down their sides and backs. They nibble and lick at all the places where there are tufts of matted hair or dead and itchy skin. Usually the horses start by standing face to face. Then they make their way along each other's sides, both working at the same time. When you see two horses grooming each other like this, you know that they're friends.

Wild horses are very sociable animals, and individuals often form an especially close bond with another member of the band. It helps to have a friend at grooming time, to get at those hard-to-reach spots!

*A swift kick works well as a last resort
to get an unruly horse in line.*

Family Life

In the wild, horses live in groups called *bands*. Every band is dominated by a *stallion,* or male horse. The rest of the band is made up of female horses, called *mares,* and their young. The group of female horses in a band is called a *harem.*

Within the band, there is a strict ranking. The stallion is the leader. Next in importance is a mare who usually is an older mare and favored by the stallion. When the band moves, she leads. The other mares follow in order, and after them come the young horses.

Each horse knows its place in the order and is careful to keep all of the lower-ranking horses in their proper places. If one horse upsets the order, the others warn it to get back where it belongs. They do that by making threatening movements with their heads and necks and laying their ears back against their heads. Sometimes, if a stubborn horse doesn't pay attention to these warnings, it may be bitten. If that doesn't work, the stallion or one of the other horses gives the offender a quick kick with its two powerful back legs.

On the Watch

A horse's eyes are extraordinary. They're big, and the pupils can open very wide to take in all available light. This means that horses can see well at night and in the daytime.

Opposite page:
*Thirsty as it may
be, this horse will
regularly pause
and raise its head
to check for
danger. Its special
eyes enable it to
view a wide area
at a glance.*

Your eyes are located at the front of your head. Although you can see to the front and to the sides, you can't see things behind you. But a horse's eyes are located toward the sides of its head. That position of the eyes enables the horse to see things in front of it, to its sides, and even behind it.

A horse's eyes are different from yours in another way, too. They don't both have to move in the same direction at the same time. Each eye moves independently. If you had eyes like a horse's, you'd be able to watch TV and look out of a window on the other side of the room at the same time! So don't be fooled the next time you observe a horse. It may seem to be concentrating only on eating, but it's also quite aware of everything else around, watching out for its neighbors or any approaching danger.

What's That?

In addition to having good eyes, horses have very good hearing. Their pointed ears turn in almost any direction to catch sounds. If two horses can't see each other, they'll sometimes sound a neigh to let each other know where they are.

Horses have super sniffers, too. They can smell odors too faint for you to detect. If you watch them closely, you'll notice that horses also are always checking the air for scents.

With senses like these, and a close family group, it's no wonder that it's difficult to sneak up on a wild horse. At the first sight, sound, or smell of anything that might be dangerous, a stallion drives his band into a tight group and sends them galloping off to safety. He stays at the rear of the group, between his band and the threat.

*Super ears, special eyes, and a keen nose
are powerful tools for spotting enemies
even at a great distance.*

Horse Talk

Like many animals, horses communicate with one another through the sounds they make. Horses whinny and neigh to each other. Usually this just means, "I'm over here." Sometimes, however, it can be a warning call.

But not all "horse talk" is done by whinnies and neighs. Horses can also send messages by the way they hold their ears. Ears pushed flat back against a horse's head are usually saying, "Don't bother me. I'm angry." If a horse's ears are quickly perked forward, it means that the horse has been startled or frightened. Horses also prick up their ears as a form of greeting.

Horses usually graze in pairs or in small groups.

Chew, Chew, Chew

Fresh green grasses are the favorite food of all horses. But in some of the places they live, wild horses must make do with other plants or leaves. They've been known to eat holly leaves, young twigs, and gorse bushes (a type of evergreen). Horses also dig with their hoofs for plant roots. On Sable Island in winter, the wild horses sometimes eat dry seaweed that they find along the beaches.

When they eat, horses crop the food off with their long, sharp front teeth and then grind it into a pulp with their flat back teeth, called *molars.* Unlike cows and other grass-eating animals, horses have very inefficient stomachs and digestive systems. They need to chew their food until it is soft and mushy before they swallow it. Since they eat up to 30 pounds (14 kilograms) of grass a day, horses sometimes spend half of their time just chewing!

A wild horse on Sable Island snacks on dry seaweed found along the seashore.

Running Shoes

If you spent a lot of time running over hard ground, you'd want a sturdy pair of shoes to protect your feet. Horses have built-in shoes—their hoofs.

You may be surprised to learn that horses walk on tiptoe and that their hoofs are actually overgrown toenails. Over thousands and thousands of years, horses' feet changed from the padded feet with toes that *Eohippus* had. Gradually, horses began to walk on one long toe. On this toe, the nail grew larger and flatter, forming a protective shoe, or hoof.

Horses that are ridden by people need man-made horseshoes because the extra weight they carry wears down their hoofs. But wild horses don't need extra shoes. Their own "running shoes" are enough protection.

Overleaf:
Wild horses can run for hours on end, spurting to a fast 35 miles (56 kilometers) per hour.

With heavy-duty shoes conveniently built in, a wild horse can enjoy a carefree and speedy gallop.

Like the Wind

When in danger, a wild horse's first reaction always is to run away. All horses love to run, and they're perfectly suited to it. They have hoofs to protect their feet and long, powerful legs to speed them onward. Their wide, flaring nostrils can take in lots of air, and they have huge *lungs,* the part of the body that takes in oxygen from the air and makes it available to the rest of the body. It is the combination of all these features that makes the horse one of the best and fastest runners in the world.

Of all horses, the thoroughbreds that run at racetracks are the fastest. Especially bred for speed, thoroughbreds have even longer legs than other horses. Over the distance of a mile or two (a few kilometers), thoroughbreds can outrun any other kind of horse.

But over long distances, a wild horse can outrun anything. It can run for hours on end, over country so rough that any other horse would probably slip or fall or just give up. Because of its speed and endurance, the wild horse has few natural enemies.

A Stallion Fight

Every spring, stallions and their mares *mate,* or come together, to produce young. When a mare is ready to mate, every stallion in the neighborhood knows it because she gives off a special scent. Very often several stallions will try to mate with the mare, so her family stallion has to fight them off.

A stallion fight often looks much more fierce than it really is. The two stallions prance toward one another with their necks arched. They toss their heads and long manes from side to side and stamp their hoofs on the ground.

A stallion's flashing eyes and laid-back ears, as well as its snorts and squeals, often are enough to make one horse retreat. If neither does, they must fight. The two stallions rear up on their hind legs and kick out their front legs. They try to knock each other over and bite each other's necks. Sometimes, if the fighting is really fierce, they may suddenly wheel around on their front legs and kick out with their very powerful hind legs.

Usually, though, one stallion gives up quite quickly. As soon as it learns that it is the weaker one, it will turn and run away. The proud victor then prances back to his harem and mates with his mare.

About 11 months after mating, the mare is ready to give birth to a foal. This almost always happens in the spring and almost always at night. Darkness helps to hide the newborn from *predators,* animals that hunt other animals for food.

Stallions fight over the right to mate with a female.

A Foal Is Born

Most of the time, a wild stallion tries to keep the mares in his harem close together to protect them from danger. But in the spring when a mare is ready to give birth, the stallion allows her to leave the group and to find a nearby sheltered spot.

The foal that is born is tiny and trembling. The name for a baby male horse is *colt*. The name for a baby female horse is *filly*.

Immediately after it's born, the baby's mother starts to lick it and nuzzle it, encouraging the delicate, spindly-legged youngster to stand up. Normally within an hour, the colt or filly can stand with its legs spread out, but it is wobbly and shaky from the effort.

Mares usually give birth to only one foal at a time.

Warm Welcome

At first, the new foal huddles close to its mother for warmth, comfort, and food. The baby *nurses,* or drinks milk from its mother's body. And in just a few hours after its birth, the baby will feel strong and more confident. Then it's ready to meet the rest of the band. The adult horses seem to be curious about the new arrival. They sniff and lick it in welcome.

Very soon, the new foal is running around, jumping and kicking up its heels, ready to gallop with the rest of the band. If there are other youngsters around, so much the better. The young foals will chase each other and play a kind of horse tag until they're exhausted or hungry and ready for another meal of their mother's milk.

Foals quickly become stronger and soon are munching on grass as well as nursing on their mother's milk. Chasing games now often end in play-fights among young colts as they practice for the stallion fights they will one day take part in.

Opposite page:
A foal runs free with its mother. If its life continues normally, it can expect to live to 20 years or more, the life span of wild horses.

Going It Alone

When they're about three years old, young stallions start to challenge their father. After a few challenges, the father becomes annoyed and chases the young stallion away. The time has come for it to fend for itself.

Very few young stallions are strong enough or smart enough to beat another stallion in a fight for a mare. Instead, they join up with other young stallions in a bachelor band. Under the leadership of the strongest, they spend much of their time play-fighting, attempting raids on other bands to try and win over a mare, and learning the skills they'll need when they're ready to start their own families.

At about the same age, young females are also driven off by their father to find a mate. The young mare quickly finds male suitors. They may include a stallion that already has a small family, or perhaps a young leader of a bachelor band. After a challenge, or perhaps a fight, the proud victor will come to claim his new mare, and they'll gallop off together to new pastures to start a new family.

Words To Know

Band   Group of horses living together.

Camouflage   Coloring and markings on an animal that help it blend in with its surroundings.

Colt   A young male horse.

Domestic   Having been tamed.

Extinct   Having gone out of existence.

Feral horses   Horses that roam wild in North America and other parts of the world.

Filly   A young female horse.

Foal   A baby horse.

Groom   To clean.

Habitat   The type of place in which an animal naturally lives.

Hand   The unit used to measure the height of a horse.

Harem   The group of mares in a band.

Hoofs   Hard nail-like growths that make up the horse's feet.

Lungs   The part of the body that takes in oxygen from the air and makes it available to the rest of the body.

Mare   A female horse.

Mate   To come together to produce young.

Molars   Flat teeth at the back of the mouth used to grind up food.

Mustangs   Wild horses, especially those living in the deserts and mountains of the West.

Nurse   To drink milk from the mother's body.

Predator   An animal that hunts other animals for food.

Stallion   A male horse.

Index

PHOTO CREDITS
Cover: Michael H. Francis, *Ivy Images*. **Interiors:** *Ivy Images:* Michael H. Francis, 4, 7, 11, 20, 23, 24, 43, 44; Alan & Sandy Carey, 19. /*Valan Photos:* Michel Bourque, 8, 31. /Fred Bruemmer, 12. /Zoe Lucas, 15, 27, 28, 33, 34, 36-37, 40-41. /United States Fish and Wildlife Service, 16.

Getting To Know...

Nature's Children

CARIBOU

Judy Ross

GROLIER
B O O K S

Facts in Brief

Classification of the Caribou

    Class: *Mammalia* (mammals)

    Order: *Artiodactyla* (cloven-hoofed mammals)

    Family: *Cervidae* (deer family)

    Genus: *Rangifer*

    Species: *Rangifer tarandus*

World distribution. Northern regions of North America, Europe, and Asia.

Habitat. Arctic tundra and/or coniferous forest.

Distinctive physical characteristics. Antlers on both males and females; small ears and tail; large feet; coloration varies with subspecies.

Habits. Lives in small bands or larger herds, depending on the time of year; is active during the day; barren-ground caribou migrate often and over great distances

Diet. Lichens, mushrooms, grasses, twigs, shrubs.

Edited by: Elizabeth Grace Zuraw
Design/Photo Editor: Nancy Norton
Photo Rights: Ivy Images

Have you ever wondered . . .

If you think that caribou look a lot like the reindeer that pull Santa's sleigh, you're right. Reindeer is the name given to caribou that live in Russia, Norway, Sweden, and Finland. There, reindeer are raised as *domestic,* or tame, animals, and many of them are, in fact, used for pulling sleds.

A caribou probably can be a little puzzling to identify. You might easily mistake one for a very large deer. But that's understandable because the caribou is a member of the deer family. A baby caribou looks very much like a baby deer— except that it doesn't have white spots.

The kind of caribou that live on flat, barren land have antlers that are larger than those of caribou that live in woodlands.

Meet the Baby

This caribou baby, called a *fawn,* has already survived the most dangerous time in its young life—the first few hours after birth. Because it lives in a *herd,* or group, the fawn must be able to keep up with all the other member of the group. If it gets left behind, it could easily be caught by a wolf. That's why caribou mothers lick and nuzzle their newborns to encourage them to get up on their wobbly legs as soon as possible after they are born.

You were probably about one year old when you started walking. But a caribou fawn can stand up when it's only one hour old! In less than two hours, it has grown strong enough to walk several miles (kilometers). And caribou fawns are fast as well as strong. A day-old fawn can run faster than a man!

To find enough food to eat, caribou must constantly be on the move. This fawn takes time off for a refreshing drink of water.

Deer Relatives

The caribou is part of a very large family—the deer family. Some relatives that live in the caribou's neighborhood are White-tailed Deer, Mule Deer, elk, and moose. All these deer relatives have certain features in common.

They all have split *hoofs,* or feet, and none of them has any top front teeth. In addition, they all have a special way of eating. They hastily swallow their food whole and store it in a special part of their stomach. Later they bring the stored food back up into their mouths and chew it leisurely.

But the most obvious similarity among deer family members is their *antlers,* hard, bony growths on their heads. All males grow and shed a new set of antlers every year. Unlike many of their deer relatives, female caribou usually grow antlers, too, but theirs aren't as large or impressive as the males'.

Opposite page:
As a caribou's antlers grow, they're covered with a furry skin called velvet. *The velvet brings nourishment to the growing antlers.*

Caribou Country

There are two kinds of caribou found in North America. One lives in forests and mountains. These are called *woodland caribou.* The others, called *barren-ground caribou,* live on the frozen *tundra*—flat, treeless areas in the Far North. Woodland caribou may not live as far north as their barren-ground cousins, but wintertime in their forest home can be mighty cold, too.

Barren-ground caribou live where the winters are long and harsh. The cold often lasts for nine months. During this time, the ground is covered with snow, and the rivers and lakes are frozen over.

Where caribou can be found in North America

10

Woodland caribou graze along a stream.

Keeping Warm

The caribou has many ways of keeping warm in winter.

It has a special double-thick fur coat that keeps body heat in and cold and wet out. The long outer hairs, called *guard hairs,* are hollow. The hollow hairs contain air, which provides some insulation, and they lie flat against the caribou's body to form a shield against rain and snow. Under the guard hairs is a layer of crinkly *underfur,* thick fur that traps the air warmed by the caribou's body.

You know how cold your nose can get on a winter day. Luckily, the caribou isn't bothered by that problem. Its nose is completely covered with hair! In fact, every part of the caribou's body is furry, even its ears and tail. And, the caribou's ears and tail are tiny for such a big animal. That way, the caribou loses less body heat through them.

The coat of the caribou is longer and denser than that of other members of the deer family.

Changing Coats

You wouldn't want to wear your winter coat all year long, would you? In summer, you'd be much too hot. Well, the caribou doesn't wear its thick fur coat all year long either. It sheds its coat in great clumps in the early summer. Although the caribou looks tattered and patchy during this *molt,* or shedding of fur, the animal is never bald. A new lightweight coat grows in as the old winter coat falls out.

Both the woodland and the barren-ground caribou are mostly brown, with white markings on their legs, belly, neck, and tail. The woodland caribou are generally a dark chocolate brown, while the barren-ground caribou are a lighter brown color.

An old male caribou, like the one in the center of this picture, can be identified by its white mane, *the long, heavy hair around its neck.*

There's nothing dainty about a caribou's feet! But the large hoofs give the animal plenty of support as it moves across snow and ground and through water.

Fabulous Feet

The caribou's feet are well designed for walking in deep snow. Its large hoofs splay out as it walks to spread its body weight over a bigger surface—a little bit the way snowshoes support a person's weight.

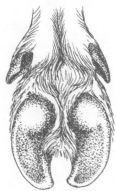

Caribou hoofs

Summer

Even ice isn't a problem for the caribou. In winter the horny edge around the outside of the animal's hoof grows. This helps the caribou dig its hoofs into ice, almost as if it were wearing cleats. At the same time, the pads in the center of the hoof shrink and harden. This way, the pads are less likely to be cut by crusty snow and ice. In addition, hair grows between the caribou's toes, forming a warm covering over the pad.

In summer the fleshy pads on the caribou's feet balloon up in size. This gives the caribou better support as it walks over soft, marshy ground.

Winter

Up Close

If a male caribou, called a *buck,* were to stand beside its enormous relative the moose, the buck would look pretty small. But it's still a fairly big animal. An average male woodland caribou weighs about 500 pounds (225 kilograms). The female, or *doe,* is quite a bit smaller.

The barren-ground caribou are considerably smaller than their woodland cousins. An average barren-ground buck weighs about 240 pounds (110 kilograms). That's about half the weight of its woodland cousin.

The size of the caribou depends on the area where it lives. In places where there's plenty of food, the caribou are bigger. Where food is scarce, the caribou are smaller. Since it's more difficult to find food in the frozen north, it isn't surprising that the barren-ground caribou of the Far North are generally smaller than the woodland variety.

If this caribou has itchy antlers, scratching them isn't going to be an easy task!

Handsome Headgear

Can you imagine carrying a couple of thick, heavy branches on top of your head all day long? That sort of thing doesn't bother a caribou at all. This animal is used to having a lot of weight on its head. A buck's thick antlers can grow as long as 3 feet (about 1 meter) and can weigh several pounds (several kilograms).

Female caribou have antlers, too, but theirs are much smaller, reaching full size when the doe is two or three years old. A buck's antlers continue to grow until he is between six and nine years old.

No two sets of caribou antlers are exactly the same. But if you look closely, you'll see that they're all made up of the same three parts. There are two heavy *beams,* or main branches, that curve back from the forehead and up; a pair of brow prongs, called *tines,* that are smaller and curve out in front; and the *shovel,* the part that curves down and over the caribou's nose.

Usually a caribou has only one shovel but

sometimes it has two. This part of the antlers probably got its name because people thought that caribou used it to shovel snow in winter when they were looking for food. We know now that this is not true. A caribou uses its front hoofs to dig for food.

Caribou shed their antlers and grow new ones every year, but males and females do so on different schedules. The bucks begin to shed their antlers in early November, although the younger bucks sometimes keep theirs until as late as January. But the females don't shed their antlers until the spring.

The buck's new antlers begin to grow in March. At first they're just fuzzy knobs. When antlers are growing in, they're covered with the furry velvet that contains blood vessels to nourish the antlers and help them grow. By mid-summer the buck's antlers stop growing, and the velvet begins to fall off. Caribou rub their antlers against trees and bushes to help get rid of this fuzzy covering.

The females grow their new set of antlers in summer, after their babies are born.

Caribou antlers

Female

Male

21

Living Together

You will hardly ever see a caribou on its own. Caribou are sociable animals and live either in small *bands,* or groups, or in large herds, depending on their type and the time of year.

Woodland caribou live in family bands that are usually made up of fewer than 50 animals. These bands change during the year. Sometimes males of the same age form a band and females form another band. Usually bands of females and males join only during the *mating season,* the time of year during which they come together to produce young.

Barren-ground caribou live in herds made up of thousands of animals.

With antlers as impressive as these, this band of caribou must be made up of bucks.

On the Move

Opposite page:
*Caribou are
known for their
swift movement.
If you ran as fast
as you could, you
might keep up
with a walking
caribou—until
you ran out
of breath.*

Some animals have homes in which they spend much of their lives. But not the caribou. They are wanderers, on the move most of the year. In the summer, they move from pasture to pasture in search of food. In the fall, they head for well-forested areas where they can find protection from the cold and snow. And in spring they travel to *birthing grounds,* special places where the young are born.

Generally, woodland caribou *migrate,* or travel from one place to another, less than barren-ground caribou. The woodland animals often move deeper into the forests or down mountains in the fall. It's their more northerly cousins who are the real wanderers.

Barren-ground caribou travel up to about 800 miles (nearly 1,300 kilometers) between their winter feeding grounds and their summer birthing grounds. They have special routes that they use every year as they move from one place to another.

A Noisy Brown Sea

People who have been lucky enough to see a large herd of barren-ground caribou migrating are amazed by the sight. They say it looks like a sea of animals passing by.

As the caribou walk or run, their legs make an odd clicking sound. This is caused when one part of a caribou's hoof rubs against another part of it. Over this clicking is the sound of antlers clashing. This clicking and clashing can sometimes be heard quite a distance away. And if there are young caribou fawns in the herd, another sound is added to the noise—loud bawling.

Caribou often travel one behind the other, following a migration route used for centuries. Older females that know the route take turns leading the way. Some herds are so large that it takes days for all of the caribou to pass!

Some migrating herds number as many as 100,000 animals. As the caribou move, other groups join them, forming a huge mass of animals.

Running and Swimming

Sometimes a herd of caribou just pokes along, but if they're alarmed, they can gallop at speeds of up to 40 miles (about 65 kilometers) an hour. But even their normal walking speed is much faster than yours.

When migrating, caribou often have to cross wide rivers or lakes. This is no problem because caribou are good swimmers. Their wide hoofs make good paddles, and their hollow, air-filled guard hairs act like a life jacket to help keep them afloat.

Caribou often cross lakes and rivers during their migrations.

Curious Caribou

We all think of cats as being curious animals, but did you know that caribou are curious, too? They don't seem to be able to resist unusual sights, such as a man waving his arms. They may run off so that they're out of danger, but then they'll turn and stare. Sometimes they'll even come back for a closer look.

Even then, their curiosity may not be fully satisfied, and they may move downwind of whatever it was that caught their attention. That's because they depend above all on their keen sense of smell to give them information about what is around them. Moving downwind allows a caribou to get a good whiff of the thing it spotted.

A caribou can spot an object or person from as far away as 400 yards (364 meters). If the object is unfamiliar, the caribou sometimes will just stand and stare at it.

Finding Food

Opposite page:
This caribou could be resting—or it could be getting ready to eat.

Caribou eat as they walk, browsing on willow shoots and nipping green buds off shrubs and leaves off plants. But the mainstay of their diet is *lichen,* a low-growing, mosslike plant that clings to rocks and trees. The average barren-ground caribou can eat about 10 pounds (4.5 kilograms) of lichen a day. For a real gourmet treat, caribou eat mushrooms.

In winter when the ground is covered with snow, caribou eat the twigs of willow and birch trees or dig down with their hoofs to find frozen bits of plants beneath the snow. Relying on their strong sense of smell, they dig under the snow to find lichen and dried horsetails, plants that are related to ferns.

Sometimes in winter, caribou even munch on muskrat homes, which are made of dried plants and grasses. It may be good food for a caribou, but what a surprise for a muskrat to find its home has been eaten!

Tear, Swallow, Grind

The caribou cannot bite off leaves or bits of lichen because it has bottom front teeth, but no top front teeth. Instead, it has a rough plate on the roof of its mouth. The caribou scrapes its front bottom teeth against the plate to tear off pieces of food. In the back of its mouth are *molars*, flattened teeth which are perfect for grinding up tough plants.

The caribou doesn't chew its food right away. It swallows lichen, leaves, and buds whole and stores them in a special part of its stomach. Later, when the caribou finds a comfortable spot to lie down, it brings the food, called *cud*, back up into its mouth and leisurely grinds it up into a pulp.

Caribou, like other deer, are called cud chewers.

Danger!

Grizzly Bears, lynx, and wolverines will all attack caribou, but wolves are their main *predators,* animals that hunt other animals for food. Groups of wolves often follow a herd of caribou, waiting to catch a fawn or a sick or old member of the herd. Only occasionally will they catch a healthy adult caribou. By keeping the caribou numbers down, wolves actually help the herd. Since they take the weaker members, there is more food for the stronger ones, who are better able to survive.

When a caribou senses danger, it lifts its head high, points its ears up, raises its tail, and holds one leg out to the side. This odd-looking pose warns other caribou, "Watch out—danger is near!" If the caribou that's given the alarm suddenly starts to run off, all the others follow, even if they haven't seen the enemy themselves.

Sometimes a frightened caribou will rear up on its hind legs like a horse. When it does, its hoofs spread apart and a special scent is deposited on the ground. Other caribou know that this smell means, "Watch out!"

Opposite page:
Head held high, ears pointing, tail raised—these are warning signs given to other caribou that an enemy is nearby.

A large group of caribou retreats to a cool snowfield to avoid insect pests in the surrounding land areas.

Pesky Pests

It may be wolves that are the biggest danger to the caribou, but flies and mosquitoes bother them the most. In the summer, the ground where barren-ground caribou live is soggy, and it has many streams and ponds where black flies and mosquitoes breed. Being bitten is an annoying but inevitable part of life for animals that live in such northern regions.

Unfortunately, the caribou's lightweight summer coat is not thick enough to protect it from bites. And its tail is not long enough to use as a fly swatter. All a caribou can do is snort with irritation and try to outrun these airborne pests. Sometimes caribou wear themselves out trying to avoid being bitten.

When the insects are out in full force, the caribou often climb up high hills or mountains to find a breezy spot with fewer bugs. If they're still being bothered, caribou will even plunge into freezing cold northern waters to escape.

Mating Time

Caribou mate in October and early November.

Opposite page: *The antler-to-antler combat of bucks is a sight seen during mating season.*

A woodland buck gathers a *harem,* or group of females, numbering about a dozen or more does. For the rest of the mating season, he will spend much of his time rushing around trying to keep them together and fighting off any other buck that tries to get near them.

Unlike their woodland cousins, male barren-ground caribou don't gather harems. Instead, they mate at random in their large herds.

Mating season is a time of great activity for the males of both caribou types. They fight with other males, bellow loudly, and sometimes even thrash their antlers around in a thicket of bushes. Before mating season, caribou bucks are fat and healthy. But they lose weight during the mating season because they don't take much time to eat. By the time winter comes, they're often tired and tattered looking.

New Life in Spring

After the long, cold winter, spring is very welcome in caribou country. The days get longer and warmer, and the does are almost ready to give birth.

Most caribou have special birthing grounds where they go to have their young. If the mother is traveling with a herd, she simply drops behind the group when it's time to have her fawn.

The fawns are born from mid-May to early June. Usually just one fawn is born, but occasionally there may be two or three. The fawn is long legged and reddish brown in color. It weighs about 10 to 13 pounds (4.5 to 6 kilograms). That's about as much as a medium-size dog weighs.

A caribou mother is very protective. She licks and cleans her newborn baby and cuddles and nuzzles it constantly. After it has rested a bit, she gently nudges it so that it will stand up and start walking.

A Fine Fawn

The fawn's hind legs look very wobbly and bent at first, but soon they straighten out. Before long it can keep up with its mother and the rest of its band or herd. And it can swim, too!

Like most babies, caribou fawns love to explore and meet other youngsters. Sometimes a fawn will wander away and get lost so the mother has to go after her baby. She can tell her youngster from a group of other look-alike fawns by its scent.

The active babies grow so fast that they double their birth weight within just ten days. They begin to graze on a few choice bits of greenery after about two weeks but continue to *nurse,* or drink milk from their mother's body, for at least a month. If the weather is very harsh, the mother will continue to nurse her fawn for a longer period of time.

During its first autumn, this caribou fawn will start to sprout antlers.

On the Move Again

Often mother caribou with fawns of the same age gather together in a band. That way they can set a walking speed that the fawns can keep up with.

By fall a fawn will be about five months old and starting to grow its first set of antlers. Soon its mother will be getting ready to mate again, and it'll be time for the herd to move to more sheltered winter areas.

The fawn will probably stay with its mother through the winter, but it will go off with other year-old fawns when the new group of babies is born in the spring.

Few caribou live to be older than four or five years in the wild. While that might seem like a very short life to us, it's time enough for a caribou to have several young of its own and walk thousands of miles (kilometers) in its constant wanderings.

Words To Know

Antlers   Hard, bony growths on the head of a caribou.

Band   A small group of animals that live or travel together.

Beam   The main heavy branch of an antler.

Birthing ground   The special place caribou go to give birth to babies.

Buck   A male caribou.

Cud   Hastily swallowed food brought back up for chewing later.

Doe   A female caribou.

Fawn   A young caribou.

Guard hairs   Long, coarse hairs in the outer layer of caribou fur.

Harem   Group of does that a buck gathers together at mating time.

Herd   A group of animals that stay together.

Lichen   A flowerless, mosslike plant that grows on rocks and trees.

Mane   Long, heavy hair around the necks of some animals.

Mate   To come together to produce young.

Migrate   To travel regularly in search of food or birthing grounds.

Molars   Flat teeth at the back of the mouth that grind food.

Molt   To shed fur, usually at the changes of seasons.

Nurse   To drink milk from a mother's body.

Predator   An animal that hunts other animals for food.

Shovel   The part of a caribou's antlers that curves down over its face.

Tine   Prong of a caribou's antlers.

Tundra   Flat, treeless land in arctic regions.

Underfur   Short, dense fur that traps body-warmed air next to an animal's body.

Velvet   Soft skin that covers a caribou's antlers while they grow.

Index

PHOTO CREDITS
Cover: Wayne Lynch, *Ivy Images*. **Interiors:** *Valan Photos:* Stephen J. Krasemann, 4, 8, 15, 19, 22-23, 25, 30, 34-35; Wayne Lankinen, 45. /Wayne Lankinen, 7, 37. /*Ivy Images*: Len Rue Jr., 11; Lowry Photo, 16; Wayne Lynch, 38, 41. /J. D. Taylor, 13, 33. /Fred Bruemmer, 26, 29, 42.